Non-Programmers Tutorial For Python

Josh Cogliati

May 10, 2016

ISBN: 978-1-387-31113-2

Abstract

Non-Programmers Tutorial For Python is a tutorial designed to be a introduction to the Python programming language. This guide is for someone with no programming experience.

If you have programmed in other languages I recommend using The Python Tutorial written by Guido van Rossum.

This document is available as LaTeX, HTML, PDF, and Postscript. Go to http://jjc.freeshell.org/easytut/ to see all these forms.

If you have any questions or comments please contact me at jjc@sdf.lonestar.org I welcome questions and comments about this tutorial. I will try to answer any questions you have as best as I can.

Thanks go to James A. Brown for writing most of the Windows install info. Thanks also to Elizabeth Cogliati for complaining enough :) about the original tutorial,(that is almost unusable for a non-programmer) for proofreading and for many ideas and comments on it. Thanks to Joe Oppegaard for writing all the exercises. Thanks to everyone I have missed.

Dedicated to Elizabeth Cogliati

CONTENTS

Intro

1.1 First things first

So, you've never programmed before. As we go through this tutorial I will attempt to teach you how to program. There really is only one way to learn to program. **You** must read code and write code. I'm going to show you lots of code. You should type in code that I show you to see what happens. Play around with it and make changes. The worst that can happen is that it won't work. When I type in code it will be formatted like this:

```
##Python is easy to learn
print "Hello, World!"
```

That's so it is easy to distinguish from the other text. To make it confusing I will also print what the computer outputs in that same font.

Now, on to more important things. In order to program in Python you need the Python software. If you don't already have the Python software go to http://www.python.org/download/ and get the proper version for your platform. Download it, read the instructions and get it installed.

1.2 Installing Python

First you need to download the appropriate file for your computer from http://www.python.org/download. Go to the 2.0 link (or newer) and then get the windows installer if you use Windows or the rpm or source if you use Unix.

The Windows installer will download to file. The file can then be run by double clicking on the icon that is downloaded. The installation will then proceed.

If you get the Unix source make sure you compile in the tk extension if you want to use IDLE.

1.3 Interactive Mode

Go into IDLE (also called the Python GUI). You should see a window that has some text like this:

```
Python 2.0 (#4, Dec 12 2000, 19:19:57)
[GCC 2.95.2 20000220 (Debian GNU/Linux)] on linux2
Type "copyright", "credits" or "license" for more information.
IDLE 0.6 -- press F1 for help
>>>
```

The >>> is Python way of telling you that you are in interactive mode. In interactive mode what you type is immediately run. Try typing 1+1 in. Python will respond with 2. Interactive mode allows you to test out and see what Python will do. If you ever feel you need to play with new Python statements go into interactive mode and try them out.

1.4   Creating and Running Programs

Go into IDLE if you are not already. Go to File then New Window. In this window type the following:

```
print "Hello, World!"
```

First save the program. Go to File then Save. Save it as 'hello.py'. (If you want you can save it to some other directory than the default.) Now that it is saved it can be run.

Next run the program by going to Run then Run Module (or if you have a older version of IDLE use Edit then Run script). This will output Hello, World! on the *Python Shell* window.

Confused still? Try this tutorial for IDLE at http://hkn.eecs.berkeley.edu/ dyoo/python/idle_intro/index.html

1.5   Using Python from the command line

If you don't want to use Python from the command line, you don't have too, just use IDLE. To get into interactive mode just type python with out any arguments. To run a program create it with a text editor (Emacs has a good python mode) and then run it with python program name.

Hello, World

2.1 What you should know

You should know how to edit programs in a text editor or IDLE, save them to disk (floppy or hard) and run them once they have been saved.

2.2 Printing

Programming tutorials since the beginning of time have started with a little program called Hello, World! So here it is:

```
print "Hello, World!"
```

If you are using the command line to run programs then type it in with a text editor, save it as 'hello.py' and run it with "python hello.py"

Otherwise go into IDLE, create a new window, and create the program as in section 1.4.

When this program is run here's what it prints:

```
Hello, World!
```

Now I'm not going to tell you this every time, but when I show you a program I recommend that you type it in and run it. I learn better when I type it in and you probably do too.

Now here is a more complicated program:

```
print "Jack and Jill went up a hill"
print "to fetch a pail of water;"
print "Jack fell down, and broke his crown,"
print "and Jill came tumbling after."
```

When you run this program it prints out:

```
Jack and Jill went up a hill
to fetch a pail of water;
Jack fell down, and broke his crown,
and Jill came tumbling after.
```

When the computer runs this program it first sees the line:

```
print "Jack and Jill went up a hill"
```

so the computer prints:

```
Jack and Jill went up a hill
```

Then the computer goes down to the next line and sees:

```
print "to fetch a pail of water;"
```

So the computer prints to the screen:

```
to fetch a pail of water;
```

The computer keeps looking at each line, follows the command and then goes on to the next line. The computer keeps running commands until it reaches the end of the program.

2.3 Expressions

Here is another program:

```
print "2 + 2 is", 2+2
print "3 * 4 is", 3 * 4
print 100 - 1, " = 100 - 1"
print "(33 + 2) / 5 + 11.5 = ",(33 + 2) / 5 + 11.5
```

And here is the output when the program is run:

```
2 + 2 is 4
3 * 4 is 12
99  = 100 - 1
(33 + 2) / 5 + 11.5 =  18.5
```

As you can see Python can turn your thousand dollar computer into a 5 dollar calculator.

Python has six basic operations for numbers:

Operation	Symbol	Example
Exponentiation	**	5 ** 2 == 25
Multiplication	*	2 * 3 == 6
Division	/	14 / 3 == 4
Remainder	%	14 % 3 == 2
Addition	+	1 + 2 == 3
Subtraction	−	4 − 3 == 1

Notice that division follows the rule, if there are no decimals to start with, there will be no decimals to end with. (Note: This will be changing in Python 2.3) The following program shows this:

```
print "14 / 3 = ",14 / 3
print "14 % 3 = ",14 % 3
print
print "14.0 / 3.0 =",14.0 / 3.0
print "14.0 % 3.0 =",14 % 3.0
print
print "14.0 / 3 =",14.0 / 3
print "14.0 % 3 =",14.0 % 3
print
print "14 / 3.0 =",14 / 3.0
print "14 % 3.0 =",14 % 3.0
print
```

With the output:

```
14 / 3 =  4
14 % 3 =  2

14.0 / 3.0 = 4.66666666667
14.0 % 3.0 = 2.0

14.0 / 3 = 4.66666666667
14.0 % 3 = 2.0

14 / 3.0 = 4.66666666667
14 % 3.0 = 2.0
```

Notice how Python gives different answers for some problems depending on whether or not there decimal values are used.

The order of operations is the same as in math:

1. parentheses ()

2. exponents **

3. multiplication *, division \, and remainder %

4. addition + and subtraction −

2.4 Talking to humans (and other intelligent beings)

Often in programming you are doing something complicated and may not in the future remember what you did. When this happens the program should probably be commented. A comment is a note to you and other programmers explaining what is happening. For example:

```
#Not quite PI, but an incredible simulation
print 22.0/7.0
```

Notice that the comment starts with a #. Comments are used to communicate with others who read the program and your future self to make clear what is complicated.

2.5 Examples

Each chapter (eventually) will contain examples of the programming features introduced in the chapter. You should at least look over them see if you understand them. If you don't, you may want to type them in and see what happens. Mess around them, change them and see what happens.

Denmark.py

```
print "Something's rotten in the state of Denmark."
print "                -- Shakespeare"
```

Output:

```
Something's rotten in the state of Denmark.
              -- Shakespeare
```

School.py

```
#This is not quite true outside of USA
# and is based on my dim memories of my younger years
print "Firstish Grade"
print "1+1 =",1+1
print "2+4 =",2+4
print "5-2 =",5-2
print
print "Thirdish Grade"
print "243-23 =",243-23
print "12*4 =",12*4
print "12/3 =",12/3
print "13/3 =",13/3," R ",13%3
print
print "Junior High"
print "123.56-62.12 =",123.56-62.12
print "(4+3)*2 =",(4+3)*2
print "4+3*2 =",4+3*2
print "3**2 =",3**2
print
```

Output:

```
Firstish Grade
1+1 = 2
2+4 = 6
5-2 = 3

Thirdish Grade
243-23 = 220
12*4 = 48
12/3 = 4
13/3 = 4  R  1

Junior High
123.56-62.12 = 61.44
(4+3)*2 = 14
4+3*2 = 10
3**2 = 9
```

2.6 Exercises

Write a program that prints your full name and your birthday as separate strings.

Write a program that shows the use of all 6 math functions.

Who Goes There?

3.1   Input and Variables

Now I feel it is time for a really complicated program. Here it is:

```
print "Halt!"
s = raw_input("Who Goes there? ")
print "You may pass,", s
```

When **I** ran it here is what **my** screen showed:

```
Halt!
Who Goes there? Josh
You may pass, Josh
```

Of course when you run the program your screen will look different because of the `raw_input` statement. When you ran the program you probably noticed (you did run the program, right?) how you had to type in your name and then press Enter. Then the program printed out some more text and also your name. This is an example of input. The program reaches a certain point and then waits for the user to input some data that the program can use later.

Of course, getting information from the user would be useless if we didn't have anywhere to put that information and this is where variables come in. In the previous program s is a variable. Variables are like a box that can store some piece of data. Here is a program to show examples of variables:

```
a = 123.4
b23 = 'Spam'
first_name = "Bill"
b = 432
c = a + b
print "a + b is", c
print "first_name is", first_name
print "Sorted Parts, After Midnight or",b23
```

And here is the output:

```
a + b is 555.4
first_name is Bill
Sorted Parts, After Midnight or Spam
```

Variables store data. The variables in the above program are a, b23, first_name, b, and c. The two basic types are strings and numbers. Strings are a sequence of letters, numbers and other characters. In this example b23 and first_name are variables that are storing strings. Spam, Bill, a + b is, and first_name is are the strings in this program. The characters are surrounded by " or '. The other type of variables are numbers.

Okay, so we have these boxes called variables and also data that can go into the variable. The computer will see a line like first_name = "Bill" and it reads it as Put the string Bill into the box (or variable) first_name. Later on it sees the statement c = a + b and it reads it as Put a + b or 123.4 + 432 or 555.4 into c.

Here is another example of variable usage:

```
a = 1
print a
a = a + 1
print a
a = a * 2
print a
```

And of course here is the output:

```
1
2
4
```

Even if it is the same variable on both sides the computer still reads it as: First find out the data to store and than find out where the data goes.

One more program before I end this chapter:

```
num = input("Type in a Number: ")
str = raw_input("Type in a String: ")
print "num =", num
print "num is a ",type(num)
print "num * 2 =",num*2
print "str =", str
print "str is a ",type(str)
print "str * 2 =",str*2
```

The output I got was:

```
Type in a Number: 12.34
Type in a String: Hello
num = 12.34
num is a  <type 'float'>
num * 2 = 24.68
str = Hello
str is a  <type 'string'>
str * 2 = HelloHello
```

Notice that `num` was gotten with `input` while `str` was gotten with `raw_input`. `raw_input` returns a string while `input` returns a number. When you want the user to type in a number use `input` but if you want the user to type in a string use `raw_input`.

The second half of the program uses `type` which tells what a variable is. Numbers are of type `int` or `float` (which are short for 'integer' and 'floating point' respectively). Strings are of type `string`. Integers and floats can be worked on by mathematical functions, strings cannot. Notice how when python multiples a number by a integer the expected thing happens. However when a string is multiplied by a integer the string has that many copies of it added i.e. `str * 2 = HelloHello`.

The operations with strings do slightly different things than operations with numbers. Here are some interative mode examples to show that some more.

```
>>> "This"+" "+"is"+" joined."
'This is joined.'
>>> "Ha, "*5
'Ha, Ha, Ha, Ha, Ha, '
>>> "Ha, "*5+"ha!"
'Ha, Ha, Ha, Ha, Ha, ha!'
>>>
```

Here is the list of some string operations:

Operation	Symbol	Example
Repetition	*	`"i"*5 == "iiiii"`
Concatenation	+	`"Hello, "+"World!" == "Hello, World!"`

3.2 Examples

Rate_times.py

```
#This programs calculates rate and distance problems
print "Input a rate and a distance"
rate = input("Rate:")
distance = input("Distance:")
print "Time:",distance/rate
```

Sample runs:

```
> python rate_times.py
Input a rate and a distance
Rate:5
Distance:10
Time: 2
> python rate_times.py
Input a rate and a distance
Rate:3.52
Distance:45.6
Time: 12.9545454545
```

Area.py

```
#This program calculates the perimeter and area of a rectangle
print "Calculate information about a rectangle"
length = input("Length:")
width = input("Width:")
print "Area",length*width
print "Perimeter",2*length+2*width
```

Sample runs:

```
> python area.py
Calculate information about a rectangle
Length:4
Width:3
Area 12
Perimeter 14
> python area.py
Calculate information about a rectangle
Length:2.53
Width:5.2
Area 13.156
Perimeter 15.46
```

temperature.py

```
#Converts Fahrenheit to Celsius
temp = input("Farenheit temperature:")
print (temp-32.0)*5.0/9.0
```

Sample runs:

```
> python temperature.py
Farenheit temperature:32
0.0
> python temperature.py
Farenheit temperature:-40
-40.0
> python temperature.py
Farenheit temperature:212
100.0
> python temperature.py
Farenheit temperature:98.6
37.0
```

3.3 Exercises

Write a program that gets 2 string variables and 2 integer variables from the user, concatenates (joins them together with no spaces) and displays the strings, then multiplies the two numbers on a new line.

Count to 10

4.1   While loops

Presenting our first control structure. Ordinarily the computer starts with the first line and then goes down from there. Control structures change the order that statements are executed or decide if a certain statement will be run. Here's the source for a program that uses the while control structure:

```
a = 0
while a < 10:
        a = a + 1
        print a
```

And here is the extremely exciting output:

```
1
2
3
4
5
6
7
8
9
10
```

(And you thought it couldn't get any worse after turning your computer into a five dollar calculator?) So what does the program do? First it sees the line a = 0 and makes a zero. Then it sees while a < 10: and so the computer checks to see if a < 10. The first time the computer sees this statement a is zero so it is less than 10. In other words while a is less than ten the computer will run the tabbed in statements.

Here is another example of the use of while:

```
a = 1
s = 0
print 'Enter Numbers to add to the sum.'
print 'Enter 0 to quit.'
while a != 0 :
        print 'Current Sum:',s
        a = input('Number? ')
        s = s + a
print 'Total Sum =',s
```

The first time I ran this program Python printed out:

```
File "sum.py", line 3
  while a != 0
               ^
SyntaxError: invalid syntax
```

I had forgotten to put the : after the while. The error message complained about that problem and pointed out where it thought the problem was with the ˆ . After the problem was fixed here was what I did with the program:

```
Enter Numbers to add to the sum.
Enter 0 to quit.
Current Sum: 0
Number? 200
Current Sum: 200
Number? -15.25
Current Sum: 184.75
Number? -151.85
Current Sum: 32.9
Number? 10.00
Current Sum: 42.9
Number? 0
Total Sum = 42.9
```

Notice how print 'Total Sum =',s is only run at the end. The while statement only affects the line that are tabbed in (a.k.a. indented). The != means does not equal so while a != 0 : means until a is zero run the tabbed in statements that are afterwards.

Now that we have while loops, it is possible to have programs that run forever. An easy way to do this is to write a program like this:

```
while 1 == 1:
     print "Help, I'm stuck in a loop."
```

This program will output Help, I'm stuck in a loop. until the heat death of the universe or you stop it. The way to stop it is to hit the Control (or Ctrl) button and 'c' (the letter) at the same time. This will kill the program. (Note: sometimes you will have to hit enter after the Control C.)

4.2 Examples

Fibonnacci.py

```
#This program calulates the fibonnacci sequence
a = 0
b = 1
count = 0
max_count = 20
while count < max_count:
    count = count + 1
    #we need to keep track of a since we change it
    old_a = a
    old_b = b
    a = old_b
    b = old_a + old_b
    #Notice that the , at the end of a print statement keeps it
    # from switching to a new line
    print old_a,
print
```

Output:

```
0 1 1 2 3 5 8 13 21 34 55 89 144 233 377 610 987 1597 2584 4181
```

Password.py

```
# Waits until a password has been entered.  Use control-C to break out with out
# the password

#Note that this must not be the password so that the
# while loop runs at least once.
password = "foobar"

#note that != means not equal
while password != "unicorn":
    password = raw_input("Password:")
print "Welcome in"
```

Sample run:

```
Password:auo
Password:y22
Password:password
Password:open sesame
Password:unicorn
Welcome in
```

Decisions

5.1   If statement

As always I believe I should start each chapter with a warm up typing exercise so here is a short program to compute the absolute value of a number:

```
n = input("Number? ")
if n < 0:
        print "The absolute value of",n,"is",-n
else:
        print "The absolute value of",n,"is",n
```

Here is the output from the two times that I ran this program:

```
Number? -34
The absolute value of -34 is 34

Number? 1
The absolute value of 1 is 1
```

So what does the computer do when when it sees this piece of code? First it prompts the user for a number with the statement `n = input("Number?   ")`. Next it reads the line `if n < 0:` If n is less than zero Python runs the line `print "The absolute value of",n,"is",-n`. Otherwise python runs the line `print "The absolute value of",n,"is",n`.

More formally Python looks at whether the *expression* `n < 0` is true or false. A `if` statement is followed by a *block* of statements that are run when the expression is true. Optionally after the `if` statement is a `else` statement. The `else` statement is run if the expression is false.

There are several different tests that a expression can have. Here is a table of all of them:

operator	function
<	less than
<=	less than or equal to
>	greater than
>=	greater than or equal to
==	equal
!=	not equal
<>	another way to say not equal

Another feature of the `if` command is the `elif` statement. It stands for else if and means if the original `if` statement is false and then the `elif` part is true do that part. Here's a example:

```
a = 0
while a < 10:
        a = a + 1
        if a > 5:
                print a," > ",5
        elif a <= 7:
                print a," <= ",7
        else:
                print "Neither test was true"
```

and the output:

```
1   <=   7
2   <=   7
3   <=   7
4   <=   7
5   <=   7
6   >  5
7   >  5
8   >  5
9   >  5
10   >   5
```

Notice how the `elif a <= 7` is only tested when the `if` statement fail to be true. `elif` allows multiple tests to be done in a single if statement.

5.2   Examples

High_low.py

```
#Plays the guessing game higher or lower
# (originally written by Josh Cogliati, improved by Quique)

#This should actually be something that is semi random like the
# last digits of the time or something else, but that will have to
# wait till a later chapter.  (Extra Credit, modify it to be random
# after the Modules chapter)
number = 78
guess = 0

while guess != number :
    guess = input ("Guess a number: ")

    if guess > number :
        print "Too high"

    elif guess < number :
            print "Too low"

print "Just right"
```

Sample run:

```
Guess a number:100
Too high
Guess a number:50
Too low
Guess a number:75
Too low
Guess a number:87
Too high
Guess a number:81
Too high
Guess a number:78
Just right
```

even.py

```
#Asks for a number.
#Prints if it is even or odd

number = input("Tell me a number: ")
if number % 2 == 0:
    print number,"is even."
elif number % 2 == 1:
    print number,"is odd."
else:
    print number,"is very strange."
```

Sample runs.

```
Tell me a number: 3
3 is odd.

Tell me a number: 2
2 is even.

Tell me a number: 3.14159
3.14159 is very strange.
```

average1.py

```python
#keeps asking for numbers until 0 is entered.
#Prints the average value.

count = 0
sum = 0.0
number = 1 #set this to something that will not exit
#            the while loop immediatly.

print "Enter 0 to exit the loop"

while number != 0:
    number = input("Enter a number:")
    count = count + 1
    sum = sum + number

count = count - 1 #take off one for the last number
print "The average was:",sum/count
```

Sample runs

```
Enter 0 to exit the loop
Enter a number:3
Enter a number:5
Enter a number:0
The average was: 4.0

Enter 0 to exit the loop
Enter a number:1
Enter a number:4
Enter a number:3
Enter a number:0
The average was: 2.66666666667
```

average2.py

```
#keeps asking for numbers until count have been entered.
#Prints the average value.

sum = 0.0

print "This program will take several numbers than average them"
count = input("How many numbers would you like to sum:")
current_count = 0

while current_count < count:
    current_count = current_count + 1
    print "Number ",current_count
    number = input("Enter a number:")
    sum = sum + number

print "The average was:",sum/count
```

Sample runs

```
This program will take several numbers than average them
How many numbers would you like to sum:2
Number  1
Enter a number:3
Number  2
Enter a number:5
The average was: 4.0

This program will take several numbers than average them
How many numbers would you like to sum:3
Number  1
Enter a number:1
Number  2
Enter a number:4
Number  3
Enter a number:3
The average was: 2.66666666667
```

5.3 Exercises

Modify the password guessing program to keep track of how many times the user has entered the password wrong. If it is more than 3 times, print "That must have been complicated."

Write a program that asks for two numbers. If the sum of the numbers is greater than 100, print "That is big number".

Write a program that asks the user their name, if they enter your name say "That is a nice name", if they enter "John Cleese" or "Michael Palin", tell them how you feel about them ;), otherwise tell them "You have a nice name".

Debugging

6.1 What is debugging?

> As soon as we started programming, we found to our surprise that it wasn't as easy to get programs right as we had thought. Debugging had to be discovered. I can remember the exact instant when I realized that a large part of my life from then on was going to be spent in finding mistakes in my own programs.
> – Maurice Wilkes discovers debugging, 1949

By now if you have been messing around with the programs you have probably found that sometimes the program does something you didn't want it to do. This is fairly common. Debugging is the process of figuring out what the computer is doing and then getting it to do what you want it to do. This can be tricky. I once spent nearly a week tracking down and fixing a bug that was caused by someone putting an x where a y should have been.

This chapter will be more abstract than previous chapters. Please tell me if it is useful.

6.2 What should the program do?

The first thing to do (this sounds obvious) is to figure out what the program should be doing if it is running correctly. Come up with some test cases and see what happens. For example, let's say I have a program to compute the perimeter of a rectangle (the sum of the length of all the edges). I have the following test cases:

width	height	perimeter
3	4	14
2	3	10
4	4	16
2	2	8
5	1	12

I now run my program on all of the test cases and see if the program does what I expect it to do. If it doesn't then I need to find out what the computer is doing.

More commonly some of the test cases will work and some will not. If that is the case you should try and figure out what the working ones have in common. For example here is the output for a perimeter program (you get to see the code in a minute):

```
Height: 3
Width: 4
perimeter =   15
```

```
Height: 2
Width: 3
perimeter =  11


Height: 4
Width: 4
perimeter =  16


Height: 2
Width: 2
perimeter =  8


Height: 5
Width: 1
perimeter =  8
```

Notice that it didn't work for the first two inputs, it worked for the next two and it didn't work on the last one. Try and figure out what is in common with the working ones. Once you have some idea what the problem is finding the cause is easier. With your own programs you should try more test cases if you need them.

6.3   What does the program do?

The next thing to do is to look at the source code. One of the most important things to do while programming is reading source code. The primary way to do this is code walkthroughs.

A code walkthrough starts at the first line, and works its way down until the program is done. `While` loops and `if` statements mean that some lines may never be run and some lines are run many times. At each line you figure out what Python has done.

Lets start with the simple perimeter program. Don't type it in, you are going to read it, not run it. The source code is:

```
height = input("Height: ")
width = input("Width: ")
print "perimeter = ",width+height+width+width
```

Question: What is the first line Python runs?

Answer: The first line is alway run first. In this case it is: `height = input("Height: ")`

Question: What does that line do?

Answer: Prints `Height:` , waits for the user to type a number in, and puts that in the variable height.

Question: What is the next line that runs?

Answer: In general, it is the next line down which is: `width = input("Width: ")`

Question: What does that line do?

Answer: Prints `Width:` , waits for the user to type a number in, and puts what the user types in the variable width.

Question: What is the next line that runs?

Answer: When the next line is not indented more or less than the current line, it is the line right afterwards, so it is: `print "perimeter = ",width+height+width+width` (It may also run a function in the current line, but thats a future chapter.)

Question: What does that line do?

Answer: First it prints `perimeter =`, then it prints `width+height+width+width`.

Question: Does `width+height+width+width` calculate the perimeter properly?

Answer: Let's see, perimeter of a rectangle is the bottom (width) plus the left side (height) plus the top (width) plus the right side (huh?). The last item should be the right side's length, or the height.

Question: Do you understand why some of the times the perimeter was calculated 'correctly'?

Answer: It was calculated correctly when the width and the height were equal.

The next program we will do a code walkthrough for is a program that is supposed to print out 5 dots on the screen. However, this is what the program is outputting:

```
.  .  .  .
```

And here is the program:

```
number = 5
while number > 1:
    print ".",
    number = number - 1
print
```

This program will be more complex to walkthrough since it now has indented portions (or control structures). Let us begin.

Question: What is the first line to be run?

Answer: The first line of the file: `number = 5`

Question: What does it do?

Answer: Puts the number 5 in the variable number.

Question: What is the next line?

Answer: The next line is: `while number > 1:`

Question: What does it do?

Answer: Well, `while` statements in general look at their expression, and if it is true they do the next indented block of code, otherwise they skip the next indented block of code.

Question: So what does it do right now?

Answer: If `number > 1` is true then the next two lines will be run.

Question: So is `number > 1`?

Answer: The last value put into `number` was 5 and `5 > 1` so yes.

Question: So what is the next line?

Answer: Since the `while` was true the next line is: `print ".",`

Question: What does that line do?

Answer: Prints one dot and since the statement ends with a `,` the next print statement will not be on a different screen line.

Question: What is the next line?

Answer: `number = number - 1` since that is following line and there are no indent changes.

Question: What does it do?

Answer: It calculates `number - 1`, which is the current value of `number` (or 5) subtracts 1 from it, and makes that the new value of number. So basically it changes `number`'s value from 5 to 4.

Question: What is the next line?

Answer: Well, the indent level decreases so we have to look at what type of control structure it is. It is a `while` loop, so we have to go back to the `while` clause which is `while number > 1:`

Question: What does it do?

Answer: It looks at the value of number, which is 4, and compares it to 1 and since `4 > 1` the while loop continues.

Question: What is the next line?

Answer: Since the while loop was true, the next line is: `print ".",`

Question: What does it do?

Answer: It prints a second dot on the line.

Question: What is the next line?

Answer: No indent change so it is: `number = number - 1`

Question: And what does it do?

Answer: It talks the current value of number (4), subtracts 1 from it, which gives it 3 and then finally makes 3 the new value of number.

Question: What is the next line?

Answer: Since there is an indent change caused by the end of the while loop, the next line is: `while number > 1:`

Question: What does it do?

Answer: It compares the current value of number (3) to 1. `3 > 1` so the while loop continues.

Question: What is the next line?

Answer: Since the while loop condition was true the next line is: `print ".",`

Question: And it does what?

Answer: A third dot is printed on the line.

Question: What is the next line?

Answer: It is: `number = number - 1`

Question: What does it do?

Answer: It takes the current value of number (3) subtracts from it 1 and makes the 2 the new value of number.

Question: What is the next line?

Answer: Back up to the start of the while loop: `while number > 1:`

Question: What does it do?

Answer: It compares the current value of number (2) to 1. Since `2 > 1` the while loop continues.

Question: What is the next line?

Answer: Since the while loop is continuing: `print "."`,

Question: What does it do?

Answer: It discovers the meaning of life, the universe and everything. I'm joking. (I had to make sure you were awake.) The line prints a fourth dot on the screen.

Question: What is the next line?

Answer: It's: `number = number - 1`

Question: What does it do?

Answer: Takes the current value of number (2) subtracts 1 and makes 1 the new value of number.

Question: What is the next line?

Answer: Back up to the while loop: `while number > 1:`

Question: What does the line do?

Answer: It compares the current value of number (1) to 1. Since `1 > 1` is false (one is not greater than one), the while loop exits.

Question: What is the next line?

Answer: Since the while loop condition was false the next line is the line after the while loop exits, or: `print`

Question: What does that line do?

Answer: Makes the screen go to the next line.

Question: Why doesn't the program print 5 dots?

Answer: The loop exits 1 dot too soon.

Question: How can we fix that?

Answer: Make the loop exit 1 dot later.

Question: And how do we do that?

Answer: There are several ways. One way would be to change the while loop to: `while number > 0:` Another way would be to change the conditional to: `number >= 1` There are a couple others.

6.4   How do I fix the program?

You need to figure out what the program is doing. You need to figure out what the program should do. Figure out what the difference between the two is. Debugging is a skill that has to be done to be learned. If you can't figure it out after an hour or so take a break, talk to someone about the problem or contemplate the lint in your navel. Come back in a while and you will probably have new ideas about the problem. Good luck.

Defining Functions

7.1 Creating Functions

To start off this chapter I am going to give you a example of what you could do but shouldn't (so don't type it in):

```
a = 23
b = -23

if a < 0:
    a = -a

if b < 0:
    b = -b

if a == b:
    print "The absolute values of", a,"and",b,"are equal"
else:
    print "The absolute values of a and b are different"
```

with the output being:

```
The absolute values of 23 and 23 are equal
```

The program seems a little repetitive. (Programmers hate to repeat things (That's what computers are for aren't they?)) Fortunately Python allows you to create functions to remove duplication. Here's the rewritten example:

```
a = 23
b = -23

def my_abs(num):
    if num < 0:
        num = -num
    return num

if my_abs(a) == my_abs(b):
    print "The absolute values of", a,"and",b,"are equal"
else:
    print "The absolute values of a and b are different"
```

with the output being:

```
The absolute values of 23 and -23 are equal
```

The key feature of this program is the `def` statement. `def` (short for define) starts a function definition. `def` is followed by the name of the function `my_abs`. Next comes a (followed by the parameter `num` (`num` is passed from the program into the function when the function is called). The statements after the `:` are executed when the function is used. The statements continue until either the indented statements end or a `return` is encountered. The `return` statement returns a value back to the place where the function was called.

Notice how the values of `a` and `b` are not changed. Functions of course can be used to repeat tasks that don't return values. Here's some examples:

```
def hello():
    print "Hello"

def area(width,height):
    return width*height

def print_welcome(name):
    print "Welcome",name

hello()
hello()

print_welcome("Fred")
w = 4
h = 5
print "width =",w,"height =",h,"area =",area(w,h)
```

with output being:

```
Hello
Hello
Welcome Fred
width = 4 height = 5 area = 20
```

That example just shows some more stuff that you can do with functions. Notice that you can use no arguments or two or more. Notice also when a function doesn't need to send back a value, a return is optional.

7.2   Variables in functions

Of course, when eliminating repeated code, you often have variables in the repeated code. These are dealt with in a special way in Python. Up till now, all variables we have see are global variables. Functions have a special type of variable called local variables. These variables only exist while the function is running. When a local variable has the same name as another variable such as a global variable, the local variable hides the other variable. Sound confusing? Well, hopefully this next example (which is a bit contrived) will clear things up.

```
a_var = 10
b_var = 15
e_var = 25

def a_func(a_var):
    print "in a_func a_var = ",a_var
    b_var = 100 + a_var
    d_var = 2*a_var
    print "in a_func b_var = ",b_var
    print "in a_func d_var = ",d_var
    print "in a_func e_var = ",e_var
    return b_var + 10

c_var = a_func(b_var)

print "a_var = ",a_var
print "b_var = ",b_var
print "c_var = ",c_var
print "d_var = ",d_var
```

The output is:

```
in a_func a_var =   15
in a_func b_var =   115
in a_func d_var =   30
in a_func e_var =   25
a_var =   10
b_var =   15
c_var =   125
d_var =
Traceback (innermost last):
  File "separate.py", line 20, in ?
    print "d_var = ",d_var
NameError: d_var
```

In this example the variables a_var, b_var, and d_var are all local variables when they are inside the function a_func. After the statement return b_var + 10 is run, they all cease to exist. The variable a_var is automatically a local variable since it is a parameter name. The variables b_var and d_var are local variables since they appear on the left of an equals sign in the function in the statements b_var = 100 + a_var and d_var = 2*a_var.

Inside of the function a_var is 15 since the function is called with a_func(b_var). Since at that point in time b_var is 15, the call to the function is a_func(15) This ends up setting a_var to 15 when it is inside of a_func.

As you can see, once the function finishes running, the local variables a_var and b_var that had hidden the global variables of the same name are gone. Then the statement print "a_var = ",a_var prints the value 10 rather than the value 15 since the local variable that hid the global variable is gone.

Another thing to notice is the NameError that happens at the end. This appears since the variable d_var no longer exists since a_func finished. All the local variables are deleted when the function exits. If you want to get something from a function, then you will have to use return something.

One last thing to notice is that the value of e_var remains unchanged inside a_func since it is not a parameter and it never appears on the left of an equals sign inside of the function a_func. When a global variable is accessed inside a function it is the global variable from the outside.

Functions allow local variables that exist only inside the function and can hide other variables that are outside the function.

7.3 Function walkthrough

TODO Move this section to a new chapter, Advanced Functions.

Now we will do a walk through for the following program:

```
def mult(a,b):
    if b == 0:
        return 0
    rest = mult(a,b - 1)
    value = a + rest
    return value

print "3*2 = ",mult(3,2)
```

Basically this program creates a positive integer multiplication function (that is far slower than the built in multiplication function) and then demonstrates this function with a use of the function.

Question: What is the first thing the program does?

Answer: The first thing done is the function mult is defined with the lines:

```
def mult(a,b):
    if b == 0:
        return 0
    rest = mult(a,b - 1)
    value = a + rest
    return value
```

This creates a function that takes two parameters and returns a value when it is done. Later this function can be run.

Question: What happens next?

Answer: The next line after the function, `print "3*2 = ",mult(3,2)` is run.

Question: And what does this do?

Answer: It prints `3*2 =` and the return value of `mult(3,2)`

Question: And what does `mult(3,2)` return?

Answer: We need to do a walkthrough of the `mult` function to find out.

Question: What happens next?

Answer: The variable a gets the value 3 assigned to it and the variable b gets the value 2 assigned to it.

Question: And then?

Answer: The line `if b == 0:` is run. Since b has the value 2 this is false so the line `return 0` is skipped.

Question: And what then?

Answer: The line `rest = mult(a,b - 1)` is run. This line sets the local variable `rest` to the value of `mult(a,b - 1)`. The value of a is 3 and the value of b is 2 so the function call is `mult(3,1)`

Question: So what is the value of `mult(3,1)` ?

Answer: We will need to run the function `mult` with the parameters 3 and 1.

Question: So what happens next?

Answer: The local variables in the *new* run of the function are set so that a has the value 3 and b has the value 1. Since these are local values these do not affect the previous values of a and b.

Question: And then?

Answer: Since b has the value 1 the if statement is false, so the next line becomes `rest = mult(a,b - 1)`.

Question: What does this line do?

Answer: This line will assign the value of `mult(3,0)` to rest.

Question: So what is that value?

Answer: We will have to run the function one more time to find that out. This time a has the value 3 and b has the value 0.

Question: So what happens next?

Answer: The first line in the function to run is `if b == 0:`. b has the value 0 so the next line to run is `return 0`

Question: And what does the line `return 0` do?

Answer: This line returns the value 0 out of the function.

Question: So?

Answer: So now we know that `mult(3,0)` has the value 0. Now we know what the line `rest = mult(a,b - 1)` did since we have run the function `mult` with the parameters 3 and 0. We have finished running `mult(3,0)` and are now back to running `mult(3,1)`. The variable `rest` gets assigned the value 0.

Question: What line is run next?

Answer: The line `value = a + rest` is run next. In this run of the function, a=3 and `rest`=0 so now `value`=3.

Question: What happens next?

Answer: The line `return value` is run. This returns 3 from the function. This also exits from the run of the function `mult(3,1)`. After `return` is called, we go back to running `mult(3,2)`.

Question: Where were we in `mult(3,2)`?

Answer: We had the variables a=3 and b=2 and were examining the line `rest = mult(a,b - 1)`.

Question: So what happens now?

Answer: The variable `rest` get 3 assigned to it. The next line `value = a + rest` sets `value` to 3+3 or 6.

Question: So now what happens?

Answer: The next line runs, this returns 6 from the function. We are now back to running the line `print "3*2 = ",mult(3,2)` which can now print out the 6.

Question: What is happening overall?

Answer: Basically we used two facts to caluclate the multipule of the two numbers. The first is that any number times 0 is 0 (x * 0 = 0). The second is that a number times another number is equal to the first number plus the first number times one less than the second number (x * y = x + x * (y - 1)). So what happens is 3*2 is first converted into 3 + 3*1. Then 3*1 is converted into 3 + 3*0. Then we know that any number times 0 is 0 so 3*0 is 0. Then we can calculate that 3 + 3*0 is 3 + 0 which is 3. Now we know what 3*1 is so we can calculate that 3 + 3*1 is 3 + 3 which is 6.

This is how the whole thing works:

```
3*2
3 + 3*1
3 + 3 + 3*0
3 + 3 + 0
3 + 3
6
```

These last two sections were recently written. If you have any comments, found any errors or think I need more/clearer explanations please email. I have been known in the past to make simple things incomprehensible. If the rest of the tutorial has made sense, but this section didn't, it is probably my fault and I would like to know. Thanks.

7.4   Examples

factorial.py

```
#defines a function that calculates the factorial

def factorial(n):
    if n <= 1:
        return 1
    return n*factorial(n-1)

print "2! = ",factorial(2)
print "3! = ",factorial(3)
print "4! = ",factorial(4)
print "5! = ",factorial(5)
```

Output:

```
2! = 2
3! = 6
4! = 24
5! = 120
```

temperature2.py

```
#converts temperature to fahrenheit or celsius

def print_options():
    print "Options:"
    print " 'p' print options"
    print " 'c' convert from celsius"
    print " 'f' convert from fahrenheit"
    print " 'q' quit the program"

def celsius_to_fahrenheit(c_temp):
    return 9.0/5.0*c_temp+32

def fahrenheit_to_celsius(f_temp):
    return (f_temp - 32.0)*5.0/9.0

choice = "p"
while choice != "q":
    if choice == "c":
        temp = input("Celsius temperature:")
        print "Fahrenheit:",celsius_to_fahrenheit(temp)
    elif choice == "f":
        temp = input("Fahrenheit temperature:")
        print "Celsius:",fahrenheit_to_celsius(temp)
    elif choice != "q":
        print_options()
    choice = raw_input("option:")
```

Sample Run:

```
> python temperature2.py
Options:
 'p' print options
 'c' convert from celsius
 'f' convert from fahrenheit
 'q' quit the program
option:c
Celsius temperature:30
Fahrenheit: 86.0
option:f
Fahrenheit temperature:60
Celsius: 15.5555555556
option:q
```

area2.py

```
#By Amos Satterlee
print
def hello():
    print 'Hello!'

def area(width,height):
    return width*height

def print_welcome(name):
    print 'Welcome,',name

name = raw_input('Your Name: ')
hello(),
print_welcome(name)
print
print 'To find the area of a rectangle,'
print 'Enter the width and height below.'
print
w = input('Width:  ')
while w <= 0:
    print 'Must be a positive number'
    w = input('Width:  ')
h = input('Height: ')
while h <= 0:
    print 'Must be a positive number'
    h = input('Height: ')
print 'Width =',w,' Height =',h,' so Area =',area(w,h)
```

Sample Run:

```
Your Name: Josh
Hello!
Welcome, Josh

To find the area of a rectangle,
Enter the width and height below.

Width:  -4
Must be a positive number
Width:  4
Height: 3
Width = 4  Height = 3  so Area = 12
```

7.5 Exercises

Rewrite the area.py program done in 3.2 to have a separate function for the area of a square, the area of a rectangle, and the area of a circle. (3.14 * radius**2). This program should include a menu interface.

Lists

8.1 Variables with more than one value

You have already seen ordinary variables that store a single value. However other variable types can hold more than one value. The simplest type is called a list. Here is a example of a list being used:

```
which_one = input("What month (1-12)? ")
months = ['January', 'February', 'March', 'April', 'May', 'June', 'July',\
          'August', 'September', 'October', 'November', 'December']
if 1 <= which_one <= 12:
        print "The month is",months[which_one - 1]
```

and a output example:

```
What month (1-12)? 3
The month is March
```

In this example the months is a list. months is defined with the lines months = ['January', 'February', 'March', 'April', 'May', 'June', 'July',\ 'August', 'September', 'October', 'November', 'December'] (Note that a \ can be used to split a long line). The [and] start and end the list with comma's (",") separating the list items. The list is used in months[which_one - 1]. A list consists of items that are numbered starting at 0. In other words if you wanted January you would use months[0]. Give a list a number and it will return the value that is stored at that location.

The statement if 1 <= which_one <= 12: will only be true if which_one is between one and twelve inclusive (in other words it is what you would expect if you have seen that in algebra).

Lists can be thought of as a series of boxes. For example, the boxes created by demolist = ['life',42, 'the universe', 6,'and',7] would look like this:

box number	0	1	2	3	4	5
demolist	'life'	42	'the universe'	6	'and'	7

Each box is referenced by its number so the statement demolist[0] would get 'life', demolist[1] would get 42 and so on up to demolist[5] getting 7.

8.2   More features of lists

The next example is just to show a lot of other stuff lists can do (for once I don't expect you to type it in, but you should probably play around with lists until you are comfortable with them.). Here goes:

```
demolist = ['life',42, 'the universe', 6,'and',7]
print 'demolist = ',demolist
demolist.append('everything')
print "after 'everything' was appended demolist is now:"
print demolist
print 'len(demolist) =', len(demolist)
print 'demolist.index(42) =',demolist.index(42)
print 'demolist[1] =', demolist[1]
#Next we will loop through the list
c = 0
while c < len(demolist):
    print 'demolist[',c,']=',demolist[c]
    c = c + 1
del demolist[2]
print "After 'the universe' was removed demolist is now:"
print demolist
if 'life' in demolist:
    print "'life' was found in demolist"
else:
    print "'life' was not found in demolist"
if 'amoeba' in demolist:
    print "'amoeba' was found in demolist"
if 'amoeba' not in demolist:
    print "'amoeba' was not found in demolist"
demolist.sort()
print 'The sorted demolist is ',demolist
```

The output is:

```
demolist =  ['life', 42, 'the universe', 6, 'and', 7]
after 'everything' was appended demolist is now:
['life', 42, 'the universe', 6, 'and', 7, 'everything']
len(demolist) = 7
demolist.index(42) = 1
demolist[1] = 42
demolist[ 0 ]= life
demolist[ 1 ]= 42
demolist[ 2 ]= the universe
demolist[ 3 ]= 6
demolist[ 4 ]= and
demolist[ 5 ]= 7
demolist[ 6 ]= everything
After 'the universe' was removed demolist is now:
['life', 42, 6, 'and', 7, 'everything']
'life' was found in demolist
'amoeba' was not found in demolist
The sorted demolist is  [6, 7, 42, 'and', 'everything', 'life']
```

This example uses a whole bunch of new functions. Notice that you can just print a whole list. Next the append function is used to add a new item to the end of the list. `len` returns how many items are in a list. The valid indexes (as in numbers that can be used inside of the []) of a list range from 0 to `len - 1`. The `index` function tell where the first location of an item is located in a list. Notice how `demolist.index(42)` returns 1 and when `demolist[1]` is run it returns 42. The line `#Next we will loop through the list` is a just a reminder to the programmer (also called a comment). Python will ignore any lines that start with a #. Next the lines:

```
c = 0
while c < len(demolist):
    print 'demolist[',c,']=',demolist[c]
    c = c + 1
```

Create a variable `c` which starts at 0 and is incremented until it reaches the last index of the list. Meanwhile the `print` statement prints out each element of the list.

The `del` command can be used to remove a given element in a list. The next few lines use the `in` operator to test if a element is in or is not in a list.

The `sort` function sorts the list. This is useful if you need a list in order from smallest number to largest or alphabetical. Note that this rearranges the list.

In summary for a list the following operations occur:

example	explanation
`list[2]`	accesses the element at index 2
`list[2] = 3`	sets the element at index 2 to be 3
`del list[2]`	removes the element at index 2
`len(list)`	returns the length of list
`"value" in list`	is true if `"value"` is an element in list
`"value" not in list`	is true if `"value"` is not an element in list
`list.sort()`	sorts list
`list.index("value")`	returns the index of the first place that `"value"` occurs
`list.append("value")`	adds an element `"value"` at the end of the list

This next example uses these features in a more useful way:

```
menu_item = 0
list = []
while menu_item != 9:
        print "--------------------"
        print "1. Print the list"
        print "2. Add a name to the list"
        print "3. Remove a name from the list"
        print "4. Change an item in the list"
        print "9. Quit"
        menu_item = input("Pick an item from the menu: ")
        if menu_item == 1:
                current = 0
                if len(list) > 0:
                        while current < len(list):
                                print current,". ",list[current]
                                current = current + 1
                else:
                        print "List is empty"
        elif menu_item == 2:
                name = raw_input("Type in a name to add: ")
                list.append(name)
        elif menu_item == 3:
                del_name = raw_input("What name would you like to remove: ")
                if del_name in list:
                        item_number = list.index(del_name)
                        del list[item_number]
                        #The code above only removes the first occurance of
                        # the name.  The code below from Gerald removes all.
                        #while del_name in list:
                        #       item_number = list.index(del_name)
                        #       del list[item_number]
                else:
                        print del_name," was not found"
        elif menu_item == 4:
                old_name = raw_input("What name would you like to change: ")
                if old_name in list:
                        item_number = list.index(old_name)
                        new_name = raw_input("What is the new name: ")
                        list[item_number] = new_name
                else:
                        print old_name," was not found"
print "Goodbye"
```

And here is part of the output:

```
--------------------
1. Print the list
2. Add a name to the list
3. Remove a name from the list
4. Change an item in the list
9. Quit

Pick an item from the menu: 2
Type in a name to add: Jack

Pick an item from the menu: 2
Type in a name to add: Jill

Pick an item from the menu: 1
0 .  Jack
1 .  Jill

Pick an item from the menu: 3
What name would you like to remove: Jack

Pick an item from the menu: 4
What name would you like to change: Jill
What is the new name: Jill Peters

Pick an item from the menu: 1
0 .  Jill Peters

Pick an item from the menu: 9
Goodbye
```

That was a long program. Let's take a look at the source code. The line `list = []` makes the variable `list` a list with no items (or elements). The next important line is `while menu_item != 9:`. This line starts a loop that allows the menu system for this program. The next few lines display a menu and decide which part of the program to run.

The section:

```
current = 0
if len(list) > 0:
        while current < len(list):
                print current,". ",list[current]
                current = current + 1
else:
        print "List is empty"
```

goes through the list and prints each name. `len(list_name)` tell how many items are in a list. If `len` returns 0 then the list is empty.

Then a few lines later the statement `list.append(name)` appears. It uses the `append` function to add a item to the end of the list. Jump down another two lines and notice this section of code:

```
item_number = list.index(del_name)
del list[item_number]
```

Here the `index` function is used to find the index value that will be used later to remove the item. `del list[item_number]` is used to remove a element of the list.

The next section

```
old_name = raw_input("What name would you like to change: ")
if old_name in list:
        item_number = list.index(old_name)
        new_name = raw_input("What is the new name: ")
        list[item_number] = new_name
else:
        print old_name," was not found"
```

uses `index` to find the `item_number` and then puts `new_name` where the `old_name` was.

Congraduations, with lists under your belt, you now know enough of the language that you could do any computations that a computer can do (this is technically known as Turing-Completness). Of course, there are still many features that are used to make your life easier.

8.3 Examples

test.py

```
## This program runs a test of knowledge

true = 1
false = 0

# First get the test questions
# Later this will be modified to use file io.
def get_questions():
    # notice how the data is stored as a list of lists
    return [["What color is the daytime sky on a clear day?","blue"],\
            ["What is the answer to life, the universe and everything?","42"],\
            ["What is a three letter word for mouse trap?","cat"]]
```

```
# This will test a single question
# it takes a single question in
# it returns true if the user typed the correct answer, otherwise false
def check_question(question_and_answer):
    #extract the question and the answer from the list
    question = question_and_answer[0]
    answer = question_and_answer[1]
    # give the question to the user
    given_answer = raw_input(question)
    # compare the user's answer to the testers answer
    if answer == given_answer:
        print "Correct"
        return true
    else:
        print "Incorrect, correct was:",answer
        return false




# This will run through all the questions
def run_test(questions):
    if len(questions) == 0:
        print "No questions were given."
        # the return exits the function
        return
    index = 0
    right = 0
    while index < len(questions):
        #Check the question
        if check_question(questions[index]):
            right = right + 1
        #go to the next question
        index = index + 1
    #notice the order of the computation, first multiply, then divide
    print "You got ",right*100/len(questions),"% right out of",len(questions)

#now lets run the questions
run_test(get_questions())
```

Sample Output:

```
What color is the daytime sky on a clear day?green
Incorrect, correct was: blue
What is the answer to life, the universe and everything?42
Correct
What is a three letter word for mouse trap?cat
Correct
You got  66 % right out of 3
```

8.4 Exercises

Expand the test.py program so it has menu giving the option of taking the test, viewing the list of questions and answers, and an option to Quit. Also, add a new question to ask, "What noise does a truly advanced machine make?" with the answer of "ping".

For Loops

And here is the new typing exercise for this chapter:

```
onetoten = range(1,11)
for count in onetoten:
        print count
```

and the ever-present output:

```
1
2
3
4
5
6
7
8
9
10
```

The output looks awfully familiar but the program code looks different. The first line uses the `range` function. The `range` function uses two arguments like this `range(start,finish)`. `start` is the first number that is produced. `finish` is one larger than the last number. Note that this program could have been done in a shorter way:

```
for count in range(1,11):
        print count
```

Here are some examples to show what happens with the `range` command:

```
>>> range(1,10)
[1, 2, 3, 4, 5, 6, 7, 8, 9]
>>> range(-32, -20)
[-32, -31, -30, -29, -28, -27, -26, -25, -24, -23, -22, -21]
>>> range(5,21)
[5, 6, 7, 8, 9, 10, 11, 12, 13, 14, 15, 16, 17, 18, 19, 20]
>>> range(21,5)
[]
```

The next line `for count in onetoten:` uses the `for` control structure. A `for` control structure looks like `for` variable in list:. list is gone through starting with the first element of the list and going to the last. As for goes through each element in a list it puts each into variable. That allows variable to be used in each successive time the for loop is run through. Here is another example (you don't have to type this) to demonstrate:

```
demolist = ['life',42, 'the universe', 6,'and',7,'everything']
for item in demolist:
    print "The Current item is:",
    print item
```

The output is:

```
The Current item is: life
The Current item is: 42
The Current item is: the universe
The Current item is: 6
The Current item is: and
The Current item is: 7
The Current item is: everything
```

Notice how the for loop goes through and sets item to each element in the list. (Notice how if you don't want print to go to the next line add a comma at the end of the statement (i.e. if you want to print something else on that line).) So, what is for good for? (groan) The first use is to go through all the elements of a list and do something with each of them. Here a quick way to add up all the elements:

```
list = [2,4,6,8]
sum = 0
for num in list:
        sum = sum + num
print "The sum is: ",sum
```

with the output simply being:

```
The sum is:   20
```

Or you could write a program to find out if there are any duplicates in a list like this program does:

```
list = [4, 5, 7, 8, 9, 1,0,7,10]
list.sort()
prev = list[0]
del list[0]
for item in list:
        if prev == item:
                print "Duplicate of ",prev," Found"
        prev = item
```

and for good measure:

```
Duplicate of  7  Found
```

Okay, so how does it work? Here is a special debugging version to help you understand (you don't need to type this in):

```
l = [4, 5, 7, 8, 9, 1,0,7,10]
print "l = [4, 5, 7, 8, 9, 1,0,7,10]","\tl:",l
l.sort()
print "l.sort()","\tl:",l
prev = l[0]
print "prev = l[0]","\tprev:",prev
del l[0]
print "del l[0]","\tl:",l
for item in l:
        if prev == item:
                print "Duplicate of ",prev," Found"
        print "if prev == item:","\tprev:",prev,"\titem:",item
        prev = item
        print "prev = item","\t\tprev:",prev,"\titem:",item
```

with the output being:

```
l = [4, 5, 7, 8, 9, 1,0,7,10]    l: [4, 5, 7, 8, 9, 1, 0, 7, 10]
l.sort()            l: [0, 1, 4, 5, 7, 7, 8, 9, 10]
prev = l[0]     prev: 0
del l[0]            l: [1, 4, 5, 7, 7, 8, 9, 10]
if prev == item:        prev: 0         item: 1
prev = item             prev: 1         item: 1
if prev == item:        prev: 1         item: 4
prev = item             prev: 4         item: 4
if prev == item:        prev: 4         item: 5
prev = item             prev: 5         item: 5
if prev == item:        prev: 5         item: 7
prev = item             prev: 7         item: 7
Duplicate of  7  Found
if prev == item:        prev: 7         item: 7
prev = item             prev: 7         item: 7
if prev == item:        prev: 7         item: 8
prev = item             prev: 8         item: 8
if prev == item:        prev: 8         item: 9
prev = item             prev: 9         item: 9
if prev == item:        prev: 9         item: 10
prev = item             prev: 10        item: 10
```

The reason I put so many `print` statements in the code was so that you can see what is happening in each line. (BTW, if you can't figure out why a program is not working, try putting in lots of print statements to you can see what is happening) First the program starts with a boring old list. Next the program sorts the list. This is so that any duplicates get put next to each other. The program then initializes a prev(ious) variable. Next the first element of the list is deleted so that the first item is not incorrectly thought to be a duplicate. Next a for loop is gone into. Each item of the list is checked to see if it is the same as the previous. If it is a duplicate was found. The value of prev is then changed so that the next time the for loop is run through prev is the previous item to the current. Sure enough, the 7 is found to be a duplicate. (Notice how \t is used to print a tab.)

The other way to use for loops is to do something a certain number of times. Here is some code to print out the first 11 numbers of the Fibonacci series:

```
a = 1
b = 1
for c in range(1,10):
        print a,
        n = a + b
        a = b
        b = n
```

with the surprising output:

```
1 1 2 3 5 8 13 21 34
```

Everything that can be done with `for` loops can also be done with `while` loops but `for` loops give a easy way to go through all the elements in a list or to do something a certain number of times.

Boolean Expressions

Here is a little example of boolean expressions (you don't have to type it in):

```
a = 6
b = 7
c = 42
print 1, a == 6
print 2, a == 7
print 3,a == 6 and b == 7
print 4,a == 7 and b == 7
print 5,not a == 7 and b == 7
print 6,a == 7 or b == 7
print 7,a == 7 or b == 6
print 8,not (a == 7 and b == 6)
print 9,not a == 7 and b == 6
```

With the output being:

```
1 1
2 0
3 1
4 0
5 1
6 1
7 0
8 1
9 0
```

What is going on? The program consists of a bunch of funny looking `print` statements. Each `print` statement prints a number and a expression. The number is to help keep track of which statement I am dealing with. Notice how each expression ends up being either 0 or 1. In Python false is written as 0 and true is written as 1. The lines:

```
print 1, a == 6
print 2, a == 7
```

print out a 1 and a 0 respectively just as expected since the first is true and the second is false. The third print, `print 3,a == 6 and b == 7`, is a little different. The operator `and` means if both the statement before and the statement after are true then the whole expression is true otherwise the whole expression is false. The next line, `print 4,a == 7 and b == 7`, shows how if part of an `and` expression is false, the whole thing is false. The behavior of `and` can be summarized as follows:

expression	result
true and true	true
true and false	false
false and true	false
false and false	false

Notice that if the first expression is false Python does not check the second expression since it knows the whole expression is false.

The next line, `print 5,not a == 7 and b == 7`, uses the `not` operator. `not` just gives the opposite of the expression (The expression could be rewritten as `print 5,a != 7 and b == 7`). Heres the table:

expression	result
not true	false
not false	true

The two following lines, `print 6,a == 7 or b == 7` and `print 7,a == 7 or b == 6`, use the `or` operator. The `or` operator returns true if the first expression is true, or if the second expression is true or both are true. If neither are true it returns false. Here's the table:

expression	result
true or true	true
true or false	true
false or true	true
false or false	false

Notice that if the first expression is true Python doesn't check the second expression since it knows the whole expression is true. This works since `or` is true if at least one half of the expression is true. The first part is true so the second part could be either false or true, but the whole expression is still true.

The next two lines, `print 8,not (a == 7 and b == 6)` and `print 9,not a == 7 and b == 6`, show that parentheses can be used to group expressions and force one part to be evaluated first. Notice that the parentheses changed the expression from false to true. This occurred since the parentheses forced the `not` to apply to the whole expression instead of just the `a == 7` portion.

Here is an example of using a boolean expression:

```
list = ["Life","The Universe","Everything","Jack","Jill","Life","Jill"]

#make a copy of the list.  See the More on Lists chapter to explain what
#[:] means.
copy = list[:]
#sort the copy
copy.sort()
prev = copy[0]
del copy[0]

count = 0

#go through the list searching for a match
while count < len(copy) and copy[count] != prev:
    prev = copy[count]
    count = count + 1

#If a match was not found then count can't be < len
#since the while loop continues while count is < len
#and no match is found
if count < len(copy):
    print "First Match: ",prev
```

And here is the output:

```
First Match:   Jill
```

This program works by continuing to check for match while count < len(copy and copy[count]. When either count is greater than the last index of copy or a match has been found the and is no longer true so the loop exits. The if simply checks to make sure that the while exited because a match was found.

The other 'trick' of and is used in this example. If you look at the table for and notice that the third entry is "false and won't check". If count >= len(copy) (in other words count < len(copy) is false) then copy[count] is never looked at. This is because Python knows that if the first is false then they both can't be true. This is known as a short circuit and is useful if the second half of the and will cause an error if something is wrong. I used the first expression (count < len(copy)) to check and see if count was a valid index for copy. (If you don't believe me remove the matches 'Jill' and 'Life', check that it still works and then reverse the order of count < len(copy) and copy[count] != prev to copy[count] != prev and count < len(copy).)

Boolean expressions can be used when you need to check two or more different things at once.

10.1   Examples

password1.py

```
## This programs asks a user for a name and a password.
# It then checks them to make sure the the user is allowed in.

name = raw_input("What is your name? ")
password = raw_input("What is the password? ")
if name == "Josh" and password == "Friday":
    print "Welcome Josh"
elif name == "Fred" and password == "Rock":
    print "Welcome Fred"
else:
    print "I don't know you."
```

Sample runs

```
What is your name? Josh
What is the password? Friday
Welcome Josh

What is your name? Bill
What is the password? Money
I don't know you.
```

10.2   Exercises

Write a program that has a user guess your name, but they only get 3 chances to do so until the program quits.

Dictionaries

This chapter is about dictionaries. Dictionaries have keys and values. The keys are used to find the values. Here is an example of a dictionary in use:

```
def print_menu():
    print '1. Print Phone Numbers'
    print '2. Add a Phone Number'
    print '3. Remove a Phone Number'
    print '4. Lookup a Phone Number'
    print '5. Quit'
    print
numbers = {}
menu_choice = 0
print_menu()
while menu_choice != 5:
    menu_choice = input("Type in a number (1-5):")
    if menu_choice == 1:
        print "Telephone Numbers:"
        for x in numbers.keys():
            print "Name: ",x," \tNumber: ",numbers[x]
        print
    elif menu_choice == 2:
        print "Add Name and Number"
        name = raw_input("Name:")
        phone = raw_input("Number:")
        numbers[name] = phone
    elif menu_choice == 3:
        print "Remove Name and Number"
        name = raw_input("Name:")
        if numbers.has_key(name):
            del numbers[name]
        else:
            print name," was not found"
    elif menu_choice == 4:
        print "Lookup Number"
        name = raw_input("Name:")
        if numbers.has_key(name):
            print "The number is",numbers[name]
        else:
            print name," was not found"
    elif menu_choice != 5:
        print_menu()
```

And here is my output:

```
1. Print Phone Numbers
2. Add a Phone Number
3. Remove a Phone Number
4. Lookup a Phone Number
5. Quit

Type in a number (1-5):2
Add Name and Number
Name:Joe
Number:545-4464
Type in a number (1-5):2
Add Name and Number
Name:Jill
Number:979-4654
Type in a number (1-5):2
Add Name and Number
Name:Fred
Number:132-9874
Type in a number (1-5):1
Telephone Numbers:
Name:  Jill      Number:  979-4654
Name:  Joe       Number:  545-4464
Name:  Fred      Number:  132-9874

Type in a number (1-5):4
Lookup Number
Name:Joe
The number is 545-4464
Type in a number (1-5):3
Remove Name and Number
Name:Fred
Type in a number (1-5):1
Telephone Numbers:
Name:  Jill      Number:  979-4654
Name:  Joe       Number:  545-4464

Type in a number (1-5):5
```

This program is similar to the name list earlier in the the chapter on lists. Heres how the program works. First the function `print_menu` is defined. `print_menu` just prints a menu that is later used twice in the program. Next comes the funny looking line `numbers = {}`. All that line does is tell Python that `numbers` is a dictionary. The next few lines just make the menu work. The lines:

```
for x in numbers.keys():
    print "Name: ",x," \tNumber: ",numbers[x]
```

go through the dictionary and print all the information. The function `numbers.keys()` returns a list that is then used by the `for` loop. The list returned by `keys` is not in any particular order so if you want it in alphabetic order it must be sorted. Similar to lists the statement `numbers[x]` is used to access a specific member of the dictionary. Of course in this case x is a string. Next the line `numbers[name] = phone` adds a name and phone number to the dictionary. If `name` had already been in the dictionary `phone` would replace whatever was there before. Next the lines:

```
    if numbers.has_key(name):
        del numbers[name]
```

see if a name is in the dictionary and remove it if it is. The function `numbers.has_key(name)` returns true if `name` is in `numbers` but other wise returns false. The line `del numbers[name]` removes the key `name` and the value associated with that key. The lines:

```
    if numbers.has_key(name):
        print "The number is",numbers[name]
```

check to see if the dictionary has a certain key and if it does prints out the number associated with it. Lastly if the menu choice is invalid it reprints the menu for your viewing pleasure.

A recap: Dictionaries have keys and values. Keys can be strings or numbers. Keys point to values. Values can be any type of variable (including lists or even dictionaries (those dictionaries or lists of course can contain dictionaries or lists themselves (scary right? :))). Here is an example of using a list in a dictionary:

```
    max_points = [25,25,50,25,100]
    assignments = ['hw ch 1','hw ch 2','quiz   ','hw ch 3','test']
    students = {'#Max':max_points}

    def print_menu():
        print "1. Add student"
        print "2. Remove student"
        print "3. Print grades"
        print "4. Record grade"
        print "5. Print Menu"
        print "6. Exit"



    def print_all_grades():
            print '\t',
            for i in range(len(assignments)):
                print assignments[i],'\t',
            print
            keys = students.keys()
            keys.sort()
            for x in keys:
                print x,'\t',
                grades = students[x]
                print_grades(grades)



    def print_grades(grades):
        for i in range(len(grades)):
            print grades[i],'\t\t',
        print
```

```
print_menu()
menu_choice = 0
while menu_choice != 6:
    print
    menu_choice = input("Menu Choice (1-6):")
    if menu_choice == 1:
        name = raw_input("Student to add:")
        students[name] = [0]*len(max_points)
    elif menu_choice == 2:
        name = raw_input("Student to remove:")
        if students.has_key(name):
            del students[name]
        else:
            print "Student: ",name," not found"
    elif menu_choice == 3:
        print_all_grades()

    elif menu_choice == 4:
        print "Record Grade"
        name = raw_input("Student:")
        if students.has_key(name):
            grades = students[name]
            print "Type in the number of the grade to record"
            print "Type a 0 (zero) to exit"
            for i in range(len(assignments)):
                print i+1,' ',assignments[i],'\t',
            print
            print_grades(grades)
            which = 1234
            while which != -1:
                which = input("Change which Grade:")
                which = which-1
                if 0 <= which < len(grades):
                    grade = input("Grade:")
                    grades[which] = grade
                elif which != -1:
                    print "Invalid Grade Number"
        else:
            print "Student not found"
    elif menu_choice != 6:
        print_menu()
```

and here is a sample output:

```
1. Add student
2. Remove student
3. Print grades
4. Record grade
5. Print Menu
6. Exit

Menu Choice (1-6):3
        hw ch 1         hw ch 2         quiz            hw ch 3         test
#Max    25              25              50              25              100



Menu Choice (1-6):6
1. Add student
2. Remove student
3. Print grades
4. Record grade
5. Print Menu
6. Exit

Menu Choice (1-6):1
Student to add:Bill



Menu Choice (1-6):4
Record Grade
Student:Bill
Type in the number of the grade to record
Type a 0 (zero) to exit
1   hw ch 1     2   hw ch 2     3   quiz        4   hw ch 3     5   test
0               0               0               0               0
Change which Grade:1
Grade:25
Change which Grade:2
Grade:24
Change which Grade:3
Grade:45
Change which Grade:4
Grade:23
Change which Grade:5
Grade:95
Change which Grade:0



Menu Choice (1-6):3
        hw ch 1         hw ch 2         quiz            hw ch 3         test
#Max    25              25              50              25              100
Bill    25              24              45              23              95

Menu Choice (1-6):6
```

Heres how the program works. Basically the variable students is a dictionary with the keys being the name of the students and the values being their grades. The first two lines just create two lists. The next line `students = {'#Max':max_points}` creates a new dictionary with the key #Max and the value is set to be `[25,25,50,25,100]` (since thats what `max_points` was when the assignment is made) (I use the key #Max since # is sorted ahead of any alphabetic characters). Next `print_menu` is defined. Next the `print_all_grades` function is defined in the lines:

```
def print_all_grades():
        print '\t',
        for i in range(len(assignments)):
            print assignments[i],'\t',
        print
        keys = students.keys()
        keys.sort()
        for x in keys:
            print x,'\t',
            grades = students[x]
            print_grades(grades)
```

Notice how first the keys are gotten out of the `students` dictionary with the `keys` function in the line `keys = students.keys()`. `keys` is a list so all the functions for lists can be used on it. Next the keys are sorted in the line `keys.sort()` since it is a list. `for` is used to go through all the keys. The grades are stored as a list inside the dictionary so the assignment `grades = students[x]` gives `grades` the list that is stored at the key x. The function `print_grades` just prints a list and is defined a few lines later.

The later lines of the program implement the various options of the menu. The line `students[name] = [0]*len(max_points)` adds a student to the key of their name. The notation `[0]*len(max_points)` just creates a array of 0's that is the same length as the `max_points` list.

The remove student entry just deletes a student similar to the telephone book example. The record grades choice is a little more complex. The grades are retrieved in the line `grades = students[name]` gets a reference to the grades of the student `name`. A grade is then recorded in the line `grades[which] = grade`. You may notice that `grades` is never put back into the students dictionary (as in no `students[name] = grades`). The reason for the missing statement is that `grades` is actually another name for `students[name]` and so changing `grades` changes `student[name]`.

Dictionaries provide a easy way to link keys to values. This can be used to easily keep track of data that is attached to various keys.

Using Modules

Here's this chapter's typing exercise (name it cal.py)[1]:

```
import calendar

year = input("Type in the year number:")
calendar.prcal(year)
```

And here is part of the output I got:

```
Type in the year number:2001
                                 2001

        January                   February                    March
Mo Tu We Th Fr Sa Su      Mo Tu We Th Fr Sa Su      Mo Tu We Th Fr Sa Su
 1  2  3  4  5  6  7                1  2  3  4                 1  2  3  4
 8  9 10 11 12 13 14       5  6  7  8  9 10 11       5  6  7  8  9 10 11
15 16 17 18 19 20 21      12 13 14 15 16 17 18      12 13 14 15 16 17 18
22 23 24 25 26 27 28      19 20 21 22 23 24 25      19 20 21 22 23 24 25
29 30 31                  26 27 28                  26 27 28 29 30 31
```

(I skipped some of the output, but I think you get the idea.) So what does the program do? The first line `import calendar` uses a new command `import`. The command `import` loads a module (in this case the `calendar` module). To see the commands available in the standard modules either look in the library reference for python (if you downloaded it) or go to `http://www.python.org/doc/current/lib/lib.html`. The calendar module is described in 5.9. If you look at the documentation lists a function called `prcal` that prints a calendar for a year. The line `calendar.prcal(year)` uses the function. In summary to use a module `import` it and then use module_name.function for functions in the module. Another way to write the program is:

```
from calendar import prcal

year = input("Type in the year number:")
prcal(year)
```

This version imports a specific function from a module. Here is another program that uses the Python Library (name it something like clock.py) (press Ctrl and the 'c' key at the same time to kill the program):

---

[1]import actually looks for a file named calendar.py and reads it in. If the file is named calendar.py and it sees a 'import calendar' it tries to read in itself which works poorly at best.

```
from time import time, ctime

prev_time = ""
while(1):
    the_time = ctime(time())
    if(prev_time != the_time):
        print "The time is:",ctime(time())
        prev_time = the_time
```

With some output being:

```
The time is: Sun Aug 20 13:40:04 2000
The time is: Sun Aug 20 13:40:05 2000
The time is: Sun Aug 20 13:40:06 2000
The time is: Sun Aug 20 13:40:07 2000
Traceback (innermost last):
  File "clock.py", line 5, in ?
    the_time = ctime(time())
KeyboardInterrupt
```

The output is infinite of course so I canceled it (or the output at least continues until Ctrl+C is pressed). The program just does a infinite loop and each time checks to see if the time has changed and prints it if it has. Notice how multiple names after the import statement are used in the line `from time import time, ctime`.

The Python Library contains many useful functions. These functions give your programs more abilities and many of them can simplify programming in Python.

12.1 Exercises

Rewrite the high_low.py program from section 5.2 to use the last two digits of time at that moment to be the 'random' number.

More on Lists

We have already seen lists and how they can be used. Now that you have some more background I will go into more detail about lists. First we will look at more ways to get at the elements in a list and then we will talk about copying them.

Here are some examples of using indexing to access a single element of an list:

```
>>> list = ['zero','one','two','three','four','five']
>>> list[0]
'zero'
>>> list[4]
'four'
>>> list[5]
'five'
```

All those examples should look familiar to you. If you want the first item in the list just look at index 0. The second item is index 1 and so on through the list. However what if you want the last item in the list? One way could be to use the `len` function like `list[len(list)-1]`. This way works since the `len` function always returns the last index plus one. The second from the last would then be `list[len(list)-2]`. There is an easier way to do this. In Python the last item is always index -1. The second to the last is index -2 and so on. Here are some more examples:

```
>>> list[len(list)-1]
'five'
>>> list[len(list)-2]
'four'
>>> list[-1]
'five'
>>> list[-2]
'four'
>>> list[-6]
'zero'
```

Thus any item in the list can be indexed in two ways: from the front and from the back.

Another useful way to get into parts of lists is using slices. Here is another example to give you an idea what they can be used for:

```
>>> list = [0,'Fred',2,'S.P.A.M.','Stocking',42,"Jack","Jill"]
>>> list[0]
0
>>> list[7]
'Jill'
>>> list[0:8]
[0, 'Fred', 2, 'S.P.A.M.', 'Stocking', 42, 'Jack', 'Jill']
>>> list[2:4]
[2, 'S.P.A.M.']
>>> list[4:7]
['Stocking', 42, 'Jack']
>>> list[1:5]
['Fred', 2, 'S.P.A.M.', 'Stocking']
```

Slices are used to return part of a list. The slice operator is in the form `list[first_index:following_index]`. The slice goes from the `first_index` to the index before the `following_index`. You can use both types of indexing:

```
>>> list[-4:-2]
['Stocking', 42]
>>> list[-4]
'Stocking'
>>> list[-4:6]
['Stocking', 42]
```

Another trick with slices is the unspecified index. If the first index is not specified the beginning of the list is assumed. If the following index is not specified the whole rest of the list is assumed. Here are some examples:

```
>>> list[:2]
[0, 'Fred']
>>> list[-2:]
['Jack', 'Jill']
>>> list[:3]
[0, 'Fred', 2]
>>> list[:-5]
[0, 'Fred', 2]
```

Here is a program example (copy and paste in the poem definition if you want):

```
poem = ["<B>","Jack","and","Jill","</B>","went","up","the","hill","to","<B>",\
"fetch","a","pail","of","</B>","water.","Jack","fell","<B>","down","and",\
"broke","</B>","his","crown","and","<B>","Jill","came","</B>","tumbling",\
"after"]

def get_bolds(list):
        true = 1
        false = 0
        ## is_bold tells whether or not the we are currently looking at
        ## a bold section of text.
        is_bold = false
        ## start_block is the index of the start of either an unbolded
        ## segment of text or a bolded segment.
        start_block = 0
        for index in range(len(list)):
                ##Handle a starting of bold text
                if list[index] == "<B>":
                        if is_bold:
                                print "Error:  Extra Bold"
                        ##print "Not Bold:",list[start_block:index]
                        is_bold = true
                        start_block = index+1
                ##Handle end of bold text
                ##Remember that the last number in a slice is the index
                ## after the last index used.
                if list[index] == "</B>":
                        if not is_bold:
                                print "Error: Extra Close Bold"
                        print "Bold [",start_block,":",index,"] ",\
                        list[start_block:index]
                        is_bold = false
                        start_block = index+1

get_bolds(poem)
```

with the output being:

```
Bold [ 1 : 4 ]   ['Jack', 'and', 'Jill']
Bold [ 11 : 15 ]  ['fetch', 'a', 'pail', 'of']
Bold [ 20 : 23 ]  ['down', 'and', 'broke']
Bold [ 28 : 30 ]  ['Jill', 'came']
```

The get_bold function takes in a list that is broken into words and token's. The tokens that it looks for are <B> which starts the bold text and <\B> which ends bold text. The function get_bold goes through and searches for the start and end tokens.

The next feature of lists is copying them. If you try something simple like:

```
>>> a = [1,2,3]
>>> b = a
>>> print b
[1, 2, 3]
>>> b[1] = 10
>>> print b
[1, 10, 3]
>>> print a
[1, 10, 3]
```

This probably looks surprising since a modification to b resulted in a being changed as well. What happened is that the statement b = a makes b a *reference* to a. This means that b can be thought of as another name for a. Hence any modification to b changes a as well. However some assignments don't create two names for one list:

```
>>> a = [1,2,3]
>>> b = a*2
>>> print a
[1, 2, 3]
>>> print b
[1, 2, 3, 1, 2, 3]
>>> a[1] = 10
>>> print a
[1, 10, 3]
>>> print b
[1, 2, 3, 1, 2, 3]
```

In this case b is not a reference to a since the expression a*2 creates a new list. Then the statement b = a*2 gives b a reference to a*2 rather than a reference to a. All assignment operations create a reference. When you pass a list as a argument to a function you create a reference as well. Most of the time you don't have to worry about creating references rather than copies. However when you need to make modifications to one list without changing another name of the list you have to make sure that you have actually created a copy.

There are several ways to make a copy of a list. The simplest that works most of the time is the slice operator since it always makes a new list even if it is a slice of a whole list:

```
>>> a = [1,2,3]
>>> b = a[:]
>>> b[1] = 10
>>> print a
[1, 2, 3]
>>> print b
[1, 10, 3]
```

Taking the slice [:] creates a new copy of the list. However it only copies the outer list. Any sublist inside is still a references to the sublist in the original list. Therefore, when the list contains lists the inner lists have to be copied as well. You could do that manually but Python already contains a module to do it. You use the deepcopy function of the copy module:

```
>>> import copy
>>> a = [[1,2,3],[4,5,6]]
>>> b = a[:]
>>> c = copy.deepcopy(a)
>>> b[0][1] = 10
>>> c[1][1] = 12
>>> print a
[[1, 10, 3], [4, 5, 6]]
>>> print b
[[1, 10, 3], [4, 5, 6]]
>>> print c
[[1, 2, 3], [4, 12, 6]]
```

First of all notice that a is an array of arrays. Then notice that when b[0][1] = 10 is run both a and b are changed, but c is not. This happens because the inner arrays are still references when the slice operator is used. However with deepcopy c was fully copied.

So, should I worry about references every time I use a function or =? The good news is that you only have to worry about references when using dictionaries and lists. Numbers and strings create references when assigned but every operation on numbers and strings that modifies them creates a new copy so you can never modify them unexpectedly. You do have to think about references when you are modifying a list or a dictionary.

By now you are probably wondering why are references used at all? The basic reason is speed. It is much faster to make a reference to a thousand element list than to copy all the elements. The other reason is that it allows you to have a function to modify the inputed list or dictionary. Just remember about references if you ever have some weird problem with data being changed when it shouldn't be.

Revenge of the Strings

And now presenting a cool trick that can be done with strings:

```
def shout(string):
    for character in string:
        print "Gimme a "+character
        print "'"+character+"'"

shout("Lose")

def middle(string):
    print "The middle character is:",string[len(string)/2]

middle("abcdefg")
middle("The Python Programming Language")
middle("Atlanta")
```

And the output is:

```
Gimme a L
'L'
Gimme a o
'o'
Gimme a s
's'
Gimme a e
'e'
The middle character is: d
The middle character is: r
The middle character is: a
```

What these programs demonstrate is that strings are similar to lists in several ways. The shout procedure shows that for loops can be used with strings just as they can be used with lists. The middle procedure shows that that strings can also use the len function and array indexes and slices. Most list features work on strings as well.

The next feature demonstrates some string specific features:

```
def to_upper(string):
    ## Converts a string to upper case
    upper_case = ""
    for character in string:
        if 'a' <= character <= 'z':
            location = ord(character) - ord('a')
            new_ascii = location + ord('A')
            character = chr(new_ascii)
        upper_case = upper_case + character
    return upper_case

print to_upper("This is Text")
```

with the output being:

```
THIS IS TEXT
```

This works because the computer represents the characters of a string as numbers from 0 to 255. Python has a function called `ord` (short for ordinal) that returns a character as a number. There is also a corresponding function called `chr` that converts a number into a character. With this in mind the program should start to be clear. The first detail is the line: `if 'a' <= character <= 'z':` which checks to see if a letter is lower case. If it is than the next lines are used. First it is converted into a location so that a=0,b=1,c=2 and so on with the line: `location = ord(character) - ord('a')`. Next the new value is found with `new_ascii = location + ord('A')`. This value is converted back to a character that is now upper case.

Now for some interactive typing exercise:

```
>>> #Integer to String
...
>>> 2
2
>>> repr(2)
'2'
>>> -123
-123
>>> repr(-123)
'-123'
>>> #String to Integer
...
>>> "23"
'23'
>>> int("23")
23
>>> "23"*2
'2323'
>>> int("23")*2
46
>>> #Float to String
...
>>> 1.23
1.23
>>> repr(1.23)
'1.23'
>>> #Float to Integer
...
>>> 1.23
1.23
>>> int(1.23)
1
>>> int(-1.23)
-1
>>> #String to Float
...
>>> float("1.23")
1.23
>>> "1.23"
'1.23'
>>> float("123")
123.0
```

If you haven't guessed already the function `repr` can convert a integer to a string and the function `int` can convert a string to an integer. The function `float` can convert a string to a float. The `repr` function returns a printable representation of something. Here are some examples of this:

```
>>> repr(1)
'1'
>>> repr(234.14)
'234.14'
>>> repr([4,42,10])
'[4, 42, 10]'
```

The `int` function tries to convert a string (or a float) into a integer. There is also a similar function called `float` that will convert a integer or a string into a float. Another function that Python has is the `eval` function. The `eval` function takes a string and returns data of the type that python thinks it found. For example:

```
>>> v=eval('123')
>>> print v,type(v)
123 <type 'int'>
>>> v=eval('645.123')
>>> print v,type(v)
645.123 <type 'float'>
>>> v=eval('[1,2,3]')
>>> print v,type(v)
[1, 2, 3] <type 'list'>
```

If you use the `eval` function you should check that it returns the type that you expect.

One useful string function is the `split` function. Here's the example:

```
>>> import string
>>> string.split("This is a bunch of words")
['This', 'is', 'a', 'bunch', 'of', 'words']
>>> string.split("First batch, second batch, third, fourth",",")
['First batch', ' second batch', ' third', ' fourth']
```

Notice how `split` converts a string into a list of strings. The string is split by spaces by default or by the optional second argument (in this case a comma).

14.1 Examples

```
#This program requires a excellent understanding of decimal numbers
def to_string(in_int):
    "Converts an integer to a string"
    out_str = ""
    prefix = ""
    if in_int < 0:
        prefix = "-"
        in_int = -in_int
    while in_int / 10 != 0:
        out_str = chr(ord('0')+in_int % 10) + out_str
        in_int = in_int / 10
    out_str = chr(ord('0')+in_int % 10) + out_str
    return prefix + out_str

def to_int(in_str):
    "Converts a string to an integer"
    out_num = 0
    if in_str[0] == "-":
        multiplier = -1
        in_str = in_str[1:]
    else:
        multiplier = 1
    for x in range(0,len(in_str)):
        out_num = out_num * 10 + ord(in_str[x]) - ord('0')
    return out_num * multiplier

print to_string(2)
print to_string(23445)
print to_string(-23445)
print to_int("14234")
print to_int("12345")
print to_int("-3512")
```

The output is:

```
2
23445
-23445
14234
12345
-3512
```

File IO

Here is a simple example of file IO:

```
#Write a file
out_file = open("test.txt","w")
out_file.write("This Text is going to out file\nLook at it and see\n")
out_file.close()

#Read a file
in_file = open("test.txt","r")
text = in_file.read()
in_file.close()

print text,
```

The output and the contents of the file test.txt are:

```
This Text is going to out file
Look at it and see
```

Notice that it wrote a file called test.txt in the directory that you ran the program from. The \n in the string tells Python to put a **n**ewline where it is.

A overview of file IO is:

1. Get a file object with the `open` function.

2. Read or write to the file object (depending on how it was opened)

3. Close it

The first step is to get a file object. The way to do this is to use the `open` function. The format is `file_object = open(filename,mode)` where `file_object` is the variable to put the file object, `filename` is a string with the filename, and `mode` is either `"r"` to read a file or `"w"` to write a file. Next the file objects functions can be called. The two most common functions are `read` and `write`. The `write` function adds a string to the end of the file. The `read` function reads the next thing in the file and returns it as a string. If no argument is given it will return the whole file (as done in the example).

Now here is a new version of the phone numbers program that we made earlier:

```
import string

true = 1
false = 0

def print_numbers(numbers):
    print "Telephone Numbers:"
    for x in numbers.keys():
        print "Name: ",x," \tNumber: ",numbers[x]
    print

def add_number(numbers,name,number):
    numbers[name] = number

def lookup_number(numbers,name):
    if numbers.has_key(name):
        return "The number is "+numbers[name]
    else:
        return name+" was not found"

def remove_number(numbers,name):
    if numbers.has_key(name):
        del numbers[name]
    else:
        print name," was not found"


def load_numbers(numbers,filename):
    in_file = open(filename,"r")
    while true:
        in_line = in_file.readline()
        if in_line == "":
            break
        in_line = in_line[:-1]
        [name,number] = string.split(in_line,",")
        numbers[name] = number
    in_file.close()

def save_numbers(numbers,filename):
    out_file = open(filename,"w")
    for x in numbers.keys():
        out_file.write(x+","+numbers[x]+"\n")
    out_file.close()


def print_menu():
    print '1. Print Phone Numbers'
    print '2. Add a Phone Number'
    print '3. Remove a Phone Number'
    print '4. Lookup a Phone Number'
    print '5. Load numbers'
    print '6. Save numbers'
    print '7. Quit'
    print
```

```
phone_list = {}
menu_choice = 0
print_menu()
while menu_choice != 7:
    menu_choice = input("Type in a number (1-7):")
    if menu_choice == 1:
        print_numbers(phone_list)
    elif menu_choice == 2:
        print "Add Name and Number"
        name = raw_input("Name:")
        phone = raw_input("Number:")
        add_number(phone_list,name,phone)
    elif menu_choice == 3:
        print "Remove Name and Number"
        name = raw_input("Name:")
        remove_number(phone_list,name)
    elif menu_choice == 4:
        print "Lookup Number"
        name = raw_input("Name:")
        print lookup_number(phone_list,name)
    elif menu_choice == 5:
        filename = raw_input("Filename to load:")
        load_numbers(phone_list,filename)
    elif menu_choice == 6:
        filename = raw_input("Filename to save:")
        save_numbers(phone_list,filename)
    elif menu_choice == 7:
        pass
    else:
        print_menu()
print "Goodbye"
```

Notice that it now includes saving and loading files. Here is some output of my running it twice:

```
> python tele2.py
1. Print Phone Numbers
2. Add a Phone Number
3. Remove a Phone Number
4. Lookup a Phone Number
5. Load numbers
6. Save numbers
7. Quit

Type in a number (1-7):2
Add Name and Number
Name:Jill
Number:1234
Type in a number (1-7):2
Add Name and Number
Name:Fred
Number:4321
Type in a number (1-7):1
Telephone Numbers:
Name:  Jill      Number:  1234
Name:  Fred      Number:  4321

Type in a number (1-7):6
Filename to save:numbers.txt
Type in a number (1-7):7
Goodbye


> python tele2.py
1. Print Phone Numbers
2. Add a Phone Number
3. Remove a Phone Number
4. Lookup a Phone Number
5. Load numbers
6. Save numbers
7. Quit

Type in a number (1-7):5
Filename to load:numbers.txt
Type in a number (1-7):1
Telephone Numbers:
Name:  Jill      Number:  1234
Name:  Fred      Number:  4321

Type in a number (1-7):7
Goodbye
```

The new portions of this program are:

```
def load_numbers(numbers,filename):
    in_file = open(filename,"r")
    while 1:
        in_line = in_file.readline()
        if len(in_line) == 0:
            break
        in_line = in_line[:-1]
        [name,number] = string.split(in_line,",")
        numbers[name] = number
    in_file.close()
```

```
def save_numbers(numbers,filename):
    out_file = open(filename,"w")
    for x in numbers.keys():
        out_file.write(x+","+numbers[x]+"\n")
    out_file.close()
```

First we will look at the save portion of the program. First it creates a file object with the command open(filename,"w"). Next it goes through and creates a line for each of the phone numbers with the command out_file.write(x+","+numbers[x]+"\n"). This writes out a line that contains the name, a comma, the number and follows it by a newline.

The loading portion is a little more complicated. It starts by getting a file object. Then it uses a while 1: loop to keep looping until a break statement is encountered. Next it gets a line with the line in_line = in_file.readline(). The readline function will return a empty string (len(string) == 0) when the end of the file is reached. The if statement checks for this and breaks out of the while loop when that happens. Of course if the readline function did not return the newline at the end of the line there would be no way to tell if an empty string was an empty line or the end of the file so the newline is left in what readline returns. Hence we have to get rid of the newline. The line in_line = in_line[:-1] does this for us by dropping the last character. Next the line [name,number] = string.split(in_line,",") splits the line at the comma into a name and a number. This is then added to the numbers dictionary.

15.1 Exercises

Now modify the grades program from section 11 so that is uses file IO to keep a record of the students.

Dealing with the imperfect (or how to handle errors)

So you now have the perfect program, it runs flawlessly, except for one detail, it will crash on invalid user input. Have no fear, for Python has a special control structure for you. It's called `try` and it tries to do something. Here is an example of a program with a problem:

```
print "Type Control C or -1 to exit"
number = 1
while number != -1:
    number = int(raw_input("Enter a number: "))
    print "You entered: ",number
```

Notice how when you enter @#& it outputs something like:

```
Traceback (innermost last):
  File "try_less.py", line 4, in ?
    number = int(raw_input("Enter a number: "))
ValueError: invalid literal for int(): @#&
```

As you can see the `int` function is unhappy with the number @#& (as well it should be). The last line shows what the problem is; Python found a `ValueError`. How can our program deal with this? What we do is first: put the place where the errors occurs in a `try` block, and second: tell Python how we want `ValueError`s handled. The following program does this:

```
print "Type Control C or -1 to exit"
number = 1
while number != -1:
    try:
        number = int(raw_input("Enter a number: "))
        print "You entered: ",number
    except ValueError:
        print "That was not a number."
```

Now when we run the new program and give it @#& it tells us "That was not a number." and continues with what it was doing before.

When your program keeps having some error that you know how to handle, put code in a `try` block, and put the way to handle the error in the `except` block.

16.1 Exercises

Update at least the phone numbers program so it doesn't crash if a user doesn't enter any data at the menu.

Chapter 16. Dealing with the imperfect (or how to handle errors)

SEVENTEEN

The End

I have run out of interest in adding more to this tutorial. However, I have put it up on Wikibooks at http://wikibooks.org/wiki/User:Jrincayc/Contents, where you can edit it and discuss it. For the moment I recommend looking at The Python Tutorial by Guido van Rossum. You should be able to understand a fair amount of it.

This tutorial is very much a work in progress. Thanks to everyone who has emailed me. If you have comments, I would recomend that you put them on the Wikibooks version (Note the discussion link on each page) so that everyone can discuss and think about them.

Happy programming, may it change your life and the world.

TODO=['errors','how to make modules','more on loops','more on strings', 'file io','how to use online help','try','pickle','anything anyone suggests that I think is a good idea']

FAQ

Can't use programs with input. If you are using IDLE then try using command line. This problem seems to be fixed in IDLE 0.6 and newer. If you are using an older version of IDLE try upgrading to Python 2.0 or newer.

Is there an update version? Yes, take a look at the wikibooks versions:
https://en.wikibooks.org/wiki/Non-Programmer's_Tutorial_for_Python_3
https://en.wikibooks.org/wiki/Non-Programmer's_Tutorial_for_Python_2.6

Is there a printable version? Yes, see the next question.

Is there a PDF or zipped version? Yes, go to http://jjc.freeshell.org/easytut/ for several different versions.

What is the tutorial written with? LATEX, see the 'easytut.tex' file.

I can't type in programs of more than one line. If the programs that you type in run as soon as you are typing them in, you need to edit a file instead of typing them in interactive mode. (Hint: interactive mode is the mode with the >>> prompt in front of it.)

My question is not answered here. Email me and ask. Please send me source code if at all relevent (even, (or maybe especially) if it doesn't work). Helpful things to include are what you were trying to do, what happened, what you expected to happen, error messages, version of Python, Operating System, and whether or not your cat was stepping on the keyboard. (The cat in my house has a fondness for space bars and control keys.)

I want to read it in a different language. There are several translations that I know of. One is in korean and is available at: http://home.hanmir.com/ johnsonj/easytut/easytut.html. Another is in Spanish and at: http://jjc.freeshell.org/easytut/easytut_es/. Another is in italian and is available at http://www.python.it/doc/tut_begin/index.html. Another is in Greek and available at http://jjc.freeshell.org/easytut/easytut_gr/. Another is in Russian and is available at http://jjc.freeshell.org/easytut/Easytut_Russian/ Several people have said they are doing a translation in other languages such as French, but I never heard back from them. If you have done a translation or know of any translations, please either send it to me or send me a link.

How do I make a GUI in Python? You can use either TKinter at http://www.python.org/topics/tkinter/ or WXPython at http://www.wxpython.org/

How do I make a game in Python? The best method is probably to use PYgame at http://pygame.org/

How do I make an exectable from a Python program? Short answer: Python is an interepreted language so that is impossible. Long answer is that something similar to an executable can be created by taking the Python interpreter and the file and joining them together and distributing that. For more on that problem see http://www.python.org/cgi-bin/faqw.py?req=all#4.28

I need help with the exercises Hint, the password program requires two variables, one to keep track of the number of times the password was typed in, and another to keep track of the last password typed in. Also you can download solutions from http://jjc.freeshell.org/easytut/

What and when was the last thing changed? 2000-Dec-16, added error handling chapter.

2000-Dec-22, Removed old install procedure.

2001-Jan-16, Fixed bug in program, Added example and data to lists section.

2001-Apr-5, Spelling, grammar, added another how to break programs, url fix for PDF version.

2001-May-13, Added chapter on debugging.

2001-Nov-11, Added exercises, fixed grammar, spelling, and hopefully improved explanations of some things.

2001-Nov-19, Added password exercise, revised references section.

2002-Feb-23, Moved 3 times password exercise, changed 1 to list in list examples question. Added a new example to Decisions chapter, added two new exercises.

2002-Mar-14, Changed abs to my_abs since python now defines a abs function.

2002-May-15, Added a faq about creating an executable. Added a comment from about the list example. Fixed typos from Axel Kleiboemer.

2002-Jun-14, Changed a program to use while true instead of while 1 to be more clear.

2002-Jul-5, Rewrote functions chapter. Modified fib program to hopefully be clearer.

2003-Jan-3, Added average examples to the decisions chapter.

2003-Jan-19, Added comment about value of a_var. Fixed mistake in average2.py program.

2003-Sep-5, Changed idle instruction to Run-¿Run Module.

www.ingramcontent.com/pod-product-compliance
Lightning Source LLC
Chambersburg PA
CBHW081142170526
45165CB00008B/2766